# The Pink Salt Trick

*A Natural Weight Loss Ritual to Burn Belly Fat, Beat Bloating, Boost Energy & Balance Hormones—With Pink Himalayan Salt Recipes, Detox Plans & Daily Reset Tools for Women*

Abigail Douglas

# Table of Contents

The Pink Salt Trick ............................................................. 1

Preface ................................................................................ 12

Introduction ...................................................................... 15

  Why the Pink Salt Trick Works ..................................... 15

    The Science Behind the Salt ..................................... 16

    Pink Salt as Your Metabolic Ally ............................. 17

    A Gentle Way to Burn Fat Without the Fight ........ 19

    What You'll Learn in This Book .............................. 21

Chapter 1 ............................................................................ 23

  Understanding the Root Causes of Weight Gain ....... 23

    Inflammation: The Silent Weight Gainer ............... 23

Bloating: Water Retention Isn't Always "Fat" ....... 25

1.3 Insulin Resistance: The Fat Storage Trigger.... 27

Cortisol and Stress Weight ...................................... 28

Emotional Eating and Hydration Imbalance .......... 30

The Salt Myth: Why You've Been Misled ............. 31

Chapter 2 ..................................................................... 34

The Pink Salt Ritual — How to Start Your Day for Fat Loss ............................................................................ 34

The Pink Salt Morning Elixir ................................. 35

How & When to Drink It ........................................ 36

Make It a Ritual, Not Just a Drink .......................... 40

How to Build It Into Your Life ............................... 41

Chapter 3 .................................................................. 43

Pink Salt Detox Water Variations (Day & Night Use)

.................................................................................. 43

Morning: Cucumber Mint Salt Flush ..................... 44

Midday: Anti-Bloat Berry Water ............................ 46

Evening: Turmeric-Pink Salt Tonic ........................ 48

Nighttime: Relaxation Salt Soaks (Internal & External) ................................................................ 50

Ritual Layering for Maximum Benefit ................... 52

Chapter 4 .................................................................. 55

The 21-Day Pink Salt Reset Plan ............................. 55

What Is the Pink Salt Reset? .................................... 55

Daily Core Routine (All 21 Days) ........................... 56

What to Expect – A Gentle Journey ........................ 58

Weekly Structure Overview ..................................... 59

Daily Tracker Prompts (Included in Companion Printables) ............................................................... 62

Tips for Maximum Results ...................................... 64

Real Talk: What If You Miss a Day? ...................... 64

Chapter 5 ....................................................................... 67

Daily and Weekly Meal Plans for Fat Loss with Pink Salt ................................................................................. 67

The Salt-Balanced Food Philosophy ....................... 68

Weekly Diet Structure .............................................. 68

Daily Sample Plan – Week 1: Beginner Focus ...... 70

Tips for Food Success ............................................... 76

Optional Add-Ons for Advanced Days ................... 76

**Chapter 6** ................................................................... 78

Pink Salt Recipes for Weight Loss and Gut Health ... 78

Electrolyte Drinks & Salt "Mocktails" ................... 79

Pink Salt Veggie Broths & Detox Soups................. 81

Bone Broths for Gut Lining Repair ....................... 84

Salted Herbal Teas for Metabolism & Mood......... 86

**Chapter 7** ................................................................... 90

Beauty & Body Rituals with Pink Salt ..................... 90

Salt Baths for Lymphatic Drainage........................ 91

Salt Scrubs for Cellulite & Skin Glow ................... 93

Underarm Detox with Pink Salt Paste ................... 95

Foot Soaks for Weight Loss, Hormone Balance & Stress ................................................................... 96

Optional Add-On: Salt-Infused Body Massage Oil 98

Summary Ritual Calendar ........................................ 98

# Chapter 8 ................................................................. 101

The Science of Salt, Stress, and the Nervous System ................................................................................ 101

Cortisol, Adrenals & Salt ...................................... 102

Belly Fat & the Stress-Salt Cycle ......................... 104

Energy Crashes, Salt, and Blood Sugar Swings .. 105

Emotional Eating & Nervous System Dysregulation ..................................................................... 107

Nervous System Repair Rituals with Salt............ 108

Chapter 9 ................................................................ 112

Troubleshooting & Adjustments ............................... 112

What If I Bloat?..................................................... 112

How Do I Stay Consistent While Traveling or Busy? ..................................................................... 114

When Should I Increase or Reduce My Salt? ....... 116

Who Should Not Follow This Plan? ..................... 118

Chapter 10 .............................................................. 121

Maintaining Results Long-Term .............................. 121

Using Pink Salt Post-Reset ................................. 122

How to Maintain Momentum (Sample Weekly Plan) ............................................................................ 122

Build Your Own Rituals ........................................ 124

Salt-Balance Eating Principles............................. 127

Pink Salt + Potassium Balance = Metabolic Magic ............................................................................ 128

Glossary of Key Terms................................................. 131

Acknowledgments....................................................... 134

Copyright © 2025 by Abigail Douglas

All rights reserved. No part of this book may be copied, reproduced, stored, or transmitted in any form or by any means—electronic, mechanical, photocopying, recording, or otherwise without prior written permission from the publisher, except for brief quotations used in reviews or scholarly works.

This book is for informational purposes only and is not intended as medical advice. Always consult with a qualified healthcare professional before beginning any wellness or dietary program.

## Disclaimer

This book is intended for informational purposes only and does not constitute medical advice. Always consult with a qualified healthcare provider before beginning any new health, nutrition, or wellness program. The author and publisher disclaim any liability for any adverse effects resulting from the use or application of the information contained herein.

# Preface

*The Pink Salt Trick: Burn Fat, Beat Bloat & Reset Your Body Naturally—No Diets, No Pills, Just One Simple Morning Ritual*

Tired of bloating, stubborn belly fat, and energy crashes? *The Pink Salt Trick* reveals the science-backed, metabolism-resetting secret behind one of the world's oldest natural healing minerals—**pink Himalayan salt**.

In this practical, beginner-friendly guide, you'll discover how a simple **morning ritual** using pink salt, lemon, and warm water can transform your digestion, calm cravings, balance hormones, and support **rapid fat loss** without restrictive diets or extreme workouts.

Whether you're struggling with **inflammation, adrenal fatigue, emotional eating**, or just want a sustainable path to **natural weight loss**, this book offers a gentle, proven solution grounded in **real wellness**, not gimmicks.

**What You'll Learn:**

- How **pink Himalayan salt** supports metabolism, detox, hydration, and gut health
- Why most women are unknowingly **salt-deficient** and how this impacts fat storage
- A complete **21-day pink salt reset plan** with meals, rituals, and hydration tools
- **Daily and weekly diet plans** using anti-inflammatory foods and salt-balanced recipes
- The truth about **electrolytes, mineral balance**, and why your body holds on to water
- Relaxing **salt bath rituals**, scrubs, and beauty formulas for slimming & stress relief
- How to use salt for **cravings, cortisol control, belly bloat**, and better sleep
- Tools, trackers, and printable planners for your personalized wellness journey

With stunning visuals, **step-by-step pink salt recipes**, and real-world detox tools, this is more than a weight loss book, it's your new daily ritual for healing from the inside out.

Whether you're a **beginner looking to reset** or a wellness pro ready to deepen your results, *The Pink Salt Trick* is your no-fad, no-stress, 100% natural path to **lasting weight loss, glowing skin, improved digestion, and renewed energy**.

# Introduction

### Why the Pink Salt Trick Works

There's something deeply sacred about morning rituals—those quiet moments before the world wakes up, when your breath is still steady, your mind uncluttered, and your body waiting for guidance.

This book is about one such ritual. A trick so simple it feels almost ancient. One that doesn't require you to starve yourself, count calories, or chase trends. It begins with a single ingredient: **Himalayan pink salt**.

You've probably seen it in elegant crystal jars at natural food stores or sprinkled on fancy dishes at upscale restaurants. But beneath its rosy hue lies something far more powerful than a gourmet garnish.

*The Himalayan Pink Salt*

## The Science Behind the Salt

Himalayan pink salt is not just sodium. It's a mineral-dense compound formed over 250 million years ago from ancient seabeds, rich with over **80 trace elements** like magnesium, potassium, calcium, iron, iodine, and zinc—each playing a vital role in cellular health, hormone balance, and metabolism.

Where most processed table salts are bleached, stripped, and laced with additives like anti-caking agents, pink salt is raw, unrefined, and remarkably **bioavailable**, meaning your body actually absorbs and uses the minerals it provides.

Why does that matter? Because modern life drains you.

Coffee dehydrates. Sugar spikes insulin. Stress floods your system with cortisol. Ultra-processed foods deplete your mineral reserves. And somewhere in the chaos, your metabolism slows, fat stores lock up, your energy crashes mid-afternoon, and you begin to feel heavy, inflamed, puffy and defeated.

## Pink Salt as Your Metabolic Ally

That's where the **Pink Salt Trick** comes in.

Taken first thing in the morning, a small dose of pink salt dissolved in warm water helps **restore electrolyte** balance, **stimulate digestion,** and **wake up the metabolism** without any stimulants. It **gently flushes the digestive tract, hydrates your cells,** and **supports adrenal glands** that may be burned out from chronic stress or poor sleep.

You may have heard that salt causes bloating or high blood pressure. But that's mostly the work of **refined table salt**—not natural salt. In fact, pink salt can actually help reduce water retention by pulling fluids into your cells (where they're needed), rather than letting them accumulate in your tissues.

It also supports proper stomach acid levels, which improves nutrient absorption and can even reduce sugar cravings by helping your body access its fuel more efficiently.

*The Bleached Table Salt vs. Pink Salt*

## A Gentle Way to Burn Fat Without the Fight

Weight loss is not about willpower. It's about *physiology*.

You don't need another diet that starves you into submission. You need rituals that **recalibrate your body's**

**natural rhythm**, restore hydration at the cellular level, and allow your system to burn fat as it was designed to.

The Pink Salt Trick is exactly that: **a daily ritual that turns on your body's natural detox and metabolism systems—gently, consistently, and sustainably.**

In just a few days, you may feel less bloated. By week two, your energy may rise and your cravings calm. And by the end of 21 days, many experience measurable fat loss, smoother digestion, mental clarity, and even improved sleep.

But this is about more than a number on the scale.

It's about building **trust** with your body again. Creating **a sacred pause each morning** that anchors your day. A moment where you drink deeply, breathe fully, and declare:

*"Today, I choose to nourish myself, not punish myself."*

*A clear hydration glass with lemon, pink salt, and water glowing in soft morning light*

## What You'll Learn in This Book

- How to use pink salt safely and effectively for detox and fat loss
- The difference between refined and natural salts—and why it matters

- Step-by-step instructions for the 21-day reset program
- Delicious fat-burning pink salt recipes for drinks, soups, broths, and tonics
- Real-life daily and weekly meal plans for beginners and pros alike
- Beauty rituals, bath recipes, and emotional reset tips using salt
- Troubleshooting guides, progress trackers, and long-term maintenance plans

You don't need fancy supplements, starvation, or another juice cleanse. You need minerals. You need hydration. You need a trick so simple, it feels like magic but is grounded in science.

So go ahead. Fill a glass. Stir in your pink salt. Step outside. Breathe deeply.

This is the beginning of your return to balance.

# Chapter 1

**Understanding the Root Causes of Weight Gain**

You've probably been told that weight gain is just about calories in versus calories out. That you need to eat less, move more, and cut out carbs. But here's the truth:

**Your body is not a bank account. It's a chemistry lab.**

Weight gain—especially the kind that sneaks up over time or refuses to budge despite effort—is often a **symptom**, not a cause. It's your body trying to protect you, buffer stress, and restore balance in a world that constantly throws it off.

Let's peel back the layers. Because once you understand what's actually going on inside your body, you'll finally stop blaming your willpower and start healing at the root.

## Inflammation: The Silent Weight

# Gainer

Inflammation is your body's way of sounding the alarm. It's supposed to be temporary activated when you get a cut, infection, or cold. But when stress, processed food, lack of sleep, or toxins keep piling on, your immune system stays "on."

That low-grade inflammation **raises cortisol**, **slows metabolism**, and causes fat to accumulate especially around the belly. It can make you feel puffy, swollen, and stiff. Over time, it leads to insulin resistance, chronic pain, and autoimmune issues.

**Pink Salt to the Rescue:**

Pink Himalayan salt contains **anti-inflammatory trace minerals** like magnesium and zinc, which calm the nervous system and help reduce oxidative stress. Its natural electrolyte balance also replenishes lost minerals that can fuel inflammation.

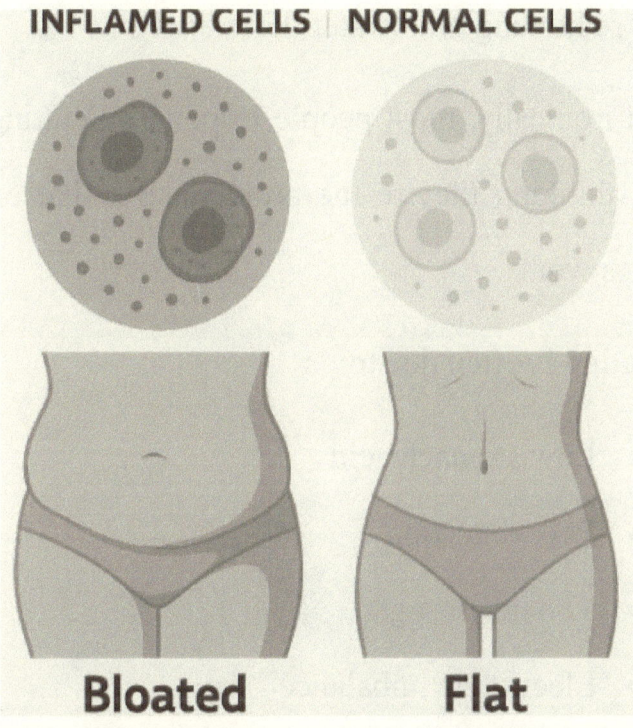

*Inflamed vs. normal body cells*

## Bloating: Water Retention Isn't Always "Fat"

Ever felt like you gained 5 pounds overnight? That's likely **bloat**, not body fat. Bloating is your body's SOS signal that something isn't digesting well, you're dehydrated, or you're holding onto water defensively.

And ironically, most people respond by cutting water or salt, thinking they're the problem. But that only makes things worse.

Bloating is often due to:

- Low stomach acid
- Poor digestion
- Too much sugar
- Electrolyte imbalance
- Overuse of processed sodium

**Pink Salt to the Rescue:**

A pinch of pink salt in warm water **stimulates digestion**, supports **stomach acid production**, and **regulates fluid balance** so water goes into your cells not around them. You feel lighter, not waterlogged.

# 1.3 Insulin Resistance: The Fat Storage Trigger

Insulin is your body's "storage hormone." Every time you eat especially sugar or refined carbs, insulin is released to help move glucose from your bloodstream into your cells.

But when you're constantly eating (especially sugar-heavy snacks), insulin remains elevated. Over time, your cells stop responding. This is called **insulin resistance**—a metabolic block that causes the body to **store fat**, especially around the waist, and struggle to burn it.

Other signs include:

- Cravings after meals
- Energy crashes
- Constant hunger
- Fatigue
- Skin tags or dark patches

**Pink Salt to the Rescue:**

Balanced electrolytes, especially from unrefined salt, **improve insulin sensitivity** by aiding cell signaling. Plus, the hydration boost from pink salt water helps stabilize blood sugar and reduce cravings.

## Cortisol and Stress Weight

Cortisol is the body's main stress hormone. It's there to protect you. But in today's world of endless deadlines, bad sleep, blue light, and processed foods, cortisol gets stuck on "high."

Chronic cortisol:

- Causes belly fat storage
- Depletes muscle
- Crashes thyroid hormones
- Increases sugar cravings
- Slows digestion and metabolism

Stress weight isn't laziness. It's biology.

**Pink Salt to the Rescue:**

Salt supports **adrenal function**, the tiny glands that produce cortisol. When you're mineral-deficient (especially in sodium and potassium), your adrenals become exhausted. Morning pink salt water gently nourishes these glands and **helps regulate stress responses**.

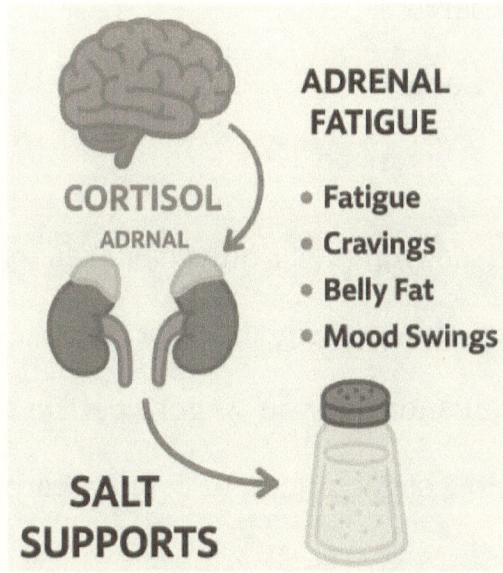

*Illustration of the brain–adrenal–cortisol connection and how salt supports it.*

# Emotional Eating and Hydration Imbalance

Let's get honest. Most of us don't eat because we're hungry. We eat because we're:

- Anxious
- Bored
- Tired
- Lonely
- Dehydrated

In fact, dehydration is often mistaken for hunger. The brain sends similar signals for both. Add emotional dysregulation and you've got a perfect storm for late-night snacking, sugar binges, or comfort carbs.

**Pink Salt to the Rescue:**

A pink salt hydration ritual can rewire the pattern. That morning drink stabilizes your mood, reduces cravings, and nourishes the body in a way that feels satisfying and grounding, even on an emotional level.

*A woman reaching for comfort food while stressed vs. sipping a warm glass of lemon-pink salt water calmly at sunrise.*

## The Salt Myth: Why You've Been Misled

"Cut back on salt." You've heard it a million times. And for those eating heavily processed foods, that advice matters. But **natural, mineral-rich salt is not the enemy**.

Here's what most health advice gets wrong:

- **Processed table salt** is stripped and chemically bleached
- It's often laced with anti-caking agents, sugars, or aluminum
- It causes water retention because it lacks balancing minerals

But **pink Himalayan salt**? It's a completely different story:

- Unprocessed
- Balanced in trace minerals
- Alkalizing
- Regulates hydration—not disrupts it

When you stop fearing salt and start understanding it, you unlock the door to **nervous system healing, hydration, digestion, and metabolism**—all key to sustainable fat loss.

**Ready for the Reset?**

You didn't gain weight overnight. And you won't lose it by cutting corners, punishing yourself, or following toxic fads. What you need is a return to rhythm. A way to support the body, not fight it.

In the next chapter, we'll start that process with a simple, beautiful ritual:

A glass of warm water, a wedge of lemon, and a pinch of nature's forgotten mineral medicine—pink salt.

# Chapter 2

## The Pink Salt Ritual — How to Start Your Day for Fat Loss

Imagine waking up every morning with a clear head, light body, and steady energy—not from coffee, but from a ritual so simple it takes less than two minutes and costs mere pennies per day. This is the **Pink Salt Morning Ritual,** and it's the heartbeat of this book.

It doesn't involve fasting.

It doesn't spike your blood sugar.

And it doesn't deplete your willpower.

Instead, it **replenishes your minerals, supports your metabolism,** and **hydrates your body at the cellular level** before you even have your first bite of food.

# The Pink Salt Morning Elixir

This is where it all begins: a glass of warm, mineral-rich, metabolism-boosting liquid sunshine. This tonic resets your nervous system, improves digestion, and activates your internal fat-burning systems all within minutes of waking.

**Classic Pink Salt Morning Elixir Recipe**

**You'll Need:**

- **8–12 oz. of warm filtered water** (not hot, not cold)
- **¼ teaspoon of high-quality pink Himalayan salt**
- **½ lemon, freshly squeezed**

**Optional Boosters (choose 1–2 based on your needs):**

- **1 tsp apple cider vinegar (ACV)** – for gut health & blood sugar balance
- **¼ tsp ground ginger** – for digestion and anti-inflammatory support

- **Pinch of cayenne pepper** – for circulation and metabolism
- **Dash of cinnamon** – for blood sugar regulation
- **1 tsp raw honey (optional)** – if you need a gentle energy lift

## How & When to Drink It

Timing is key. Your body is most **receptive and dehydrated** first thing in the morning. You've just gone 6–8 hours without water, and your cortisol is naturally rising to help you wake up.

This is when your **cells are ready to absorb minerals**, flush toxins, and recalibrate your hydration. Drinking this elixir **before coffee, food, or even exercise** gives your body a clean, energized foundation for the day.

**Daily Ritual Instructions:**

1. Warm up your water (not boiling—think bath temperature).
2. Stir in the pink salt until dissolved.
3. Squeeze in the lemon juice and add your chosen boosters.
4. Sip slowly on an empty stomach, preferably while sitting calmly and breathing deeply.

**Why This Works**

- **Salt** contains essential electrolytes like sodium, magnesium, and potassium that **regulate fluid balance, support adrenal health**, and **activate digestion**.
- **Lemon** is alkaline-forming, rich in vitamin C, and helps the liver detox gently.
- **Warm water** encourages movement through the gut, supports lymph drainage, and hydrates at the cellular level.

- **Apple cider vinegar** supports digestion, bile flow, and stable blood sugar.
- **Cayenne and ginger** gently stimulate thermogenesis—your body's heat and fat-burning system.

Together, this drink mimics the natural minerals found in our blood plasma. That's why so many people say it makes them feel calm, clear, and energized—even before breakfast.

**Safe Dosage Guidelines**

Like any tool, pink salt must be used wisely. More is **not** better. Start slow and listen to your body.

**Beginners**

- ¼ tsp of pink salt per 8 oz of water (once a day)
- Optional: Add only lemon for the first 3–5 days

- Skip vinegar or cayenne at first if sensitive

**Intermediate**

- ¼ tsp pink salt with lemon + 1 optional booster (ACV or ginger)
- Sip once daily, optionally mid-afternoon if fatigue hits

**Advanced Users**

- ¼–½ tsp pink salt with lemon + ACV + ginger or cayenne
- Optionally take a second dose mid-morning or post-workout
- Great during low-carb, detox, or adrenal support phases

**Important Notes:**

- Avoid if on a sodium-restricted diet or if you have kidney conditions.

- Always consult a health practitioner if you have hypertension or cardiovascular concerns.
- Do **not** use standard table salt—only high-quality **unrefined pink Himalayan salt** or **Celtic sea salt**.

## Make It a Ritual, Not Just a Drink

This isn't just about what's in the glass. It's about the moment.

Take a breath. Step outside if you can. Stand in the sun. Hold your warm glass and feel its weight. Sip slowly and tell your body, *"I'm here. I'm listening. I choose nourishment."*

Ritual makes habit sacred.

And sacred habits are the ones that change us.

*The final drink on a rustic morning table with a soft sunrise glow in the background*

## How to Build It Into Your Life

Here's how readers have built this ritual effortlessly:

- Pair it with journaling or meditation
- Drink it during a morning walk
- Make a big jar of it the night before
- Incorporate it into your pre-workout or yoga prep

Within days, you may notice:

- Reduced cravings
- Better digestion
- Calmer energy
- Fewer mood swings
- Less bloat and puffiness

Next, we'll explore how to keep the benefits going all day long with **detox water variations** and **midday pink salt rituals** that continue the fat-burning, anti-bloat magic. But first, lock in this one.

Tomorrow morning, your glass awaits.

# Chapter 3

**Pink Salt Detox Water Variations (Day & Night Use)**

The beauty of pink salt is that it doesn't just shine in the morning. Used wisely, it becomes a silent partner in your healing and energy all day long.

By simply infusing your water with carefully selected herbs, fruits, and spices plus a touch of pink salt—you unlock a powerful tool for fat-burning, de-bloating, skin clarity, mineral support, and even sleep enhancement.

These are not just "flavored waters." These are functional tonics, designed to work with your body's **circadian rhythm** which governs digestion, detoxification, and fat metabolism.

Let's walk through four daily blends, designed to support your body from sunrise to sleep.

# Morning: Cucumber Mint Salt Flush

**Purpose:**

Hydration, bloat relief, lymphatic drainage, digestive awakening

This crisp, cooling detox water gently stimulates your system, reduces puffiness, and refreshes your cells. Cucumber is a natural diuretic, mint supports digestion, and the salt restores lost minerals from overnight detox.

**Ingredients (per mason jar):**

- 3–5 slices of fresh cucumber
- 3–4 fresh mint leaves
- ⅛ tsp pink Himalayan salt
- Juice of ¼ lemon (optional)
- 16 oz. filtered water

**Instructions:**

- Combine ingredients in a glass jar or bottle.

- Let it infuse for 15–30 minutes before sipping.
- Best consumed within 2 hours of making.

**Pro Tip:**

*Drink this after your morning elixir, especially on hot days or when feeling puffy or groggy.*

*A mason jar with cucumber ribbons, floating mint, and light pinkish hue from salt.*

# Midday: Anti-Bloat Berry Water

**Purpose:**

Beat cravings, fight inflammation, support digestion and skin glow

This fruity blend is both delicious and therapeutic. Berries are antioxidant-rich, lemon supports liver function, and a pinch of pink salt helps regulate fluid balance, so you don't bloat after lunch.

**Ingredients (per 16 oz. jar):**

- 4–5 sliced strawberries or raspberries
- Juice of ½ lemon
- ⅛ tsp pink Himalayan salt
- 2–3 fresh basil or mint leaves (optional)
- Filtered water

**Instructions:**

- Lightly crush berries to release flavor.

- Add lemon juice, herbs, and salt.
- Let infuse at room temperature or chill for 30 mins.

*Pro Tip: Sip between meals to prevent energy crashes and reduce cravings for sweets.*

**Bright pink-hued mason jar with fresh berries and herbs inside.**

# Evening: Turmeric-Pink Salt Tonic

**Purpose:**

Reduce inflammation, soothe digestion, calm the nervous system

This golden blend is your **gentle anti-inflammatory** nightcap. Turmeric reduces pain and cortisol, pink salt provides minerals that ease muscle tension, and warm water prepares the body for sleep.

**Ingredients (1 mug):**

- 8 oz warm filtered water
- ¼ tsp turmeric powder or fresh grated turmeric
- ⅛ tsp pink salt
- Dash of black pepper (boosts turmeric absorption)
- Optional: 1 tsp raw honey or coconut oil for richness

**Instructions:**

- Mix all ingredients in warm water until dissolved.
- Stir and sip slowly before bedtime.

**Pro Tip:**

*Drink after dinner or before your evening bath for a deeply calming effect.*

*Rustic ceramic mug filled with golden liquid, pink salt visible nearby, candlelight ambiance.*

# Nighttime: Relaxation Salt Soaks (Internal & External)

You don't just drink pink salt. You can **soak in it**, too.

When added to baths or used in salt foot soaks, pink salt draws toxins from tissues, eases muscle fatigue, and balances magnesium levels. It also softens skin and prepares the body for deep sleep.

**Internal Soak (Sleep Water):**

**Ingredients:**

- 6–8 oz warm water
- ⅛ tsp pink salt
- 1 tsp raw honey or chamomile tea (optional)

**Instructions:**

- Stir and drink 30–60 minutes before bed.

This gently sedates the nervous system and replenishes

minerals that regulate melatonin and GABA (your sleep neurotransmitter).

**External Soak (Bath or Foot Soak):**

**Ingredients:**

- 1 cup pink Himalayan salt
- 5 drops lavender or eucalyptus oil
- Optional: ½ cup baking soda or magnesium flakes

**Instructions:**

- Add to warm bath or basin.
- Soak for 20–30 minutes.

Your body absorbs trace minerals transdermally, while the heat opens pores and calms your nerves.

*Glass jar of pink salt near a bathtub with lit candles.*

## Ritual Layering for Maximum Benefit

Here's how to stack these waters into a full-day detox flow:

| Time | Ritual | Result |
|---|---|---|
| **Morning** | Pink Salt Elixir + Cucumber Mint Flush | Wake up digestion, de-puff, energize |
| **Midday** | Berry Anti-Bloat Water | Prevent afternoon crash, flatten tummy |
| **Evening** | Turmeric Salt Tonic + Internal Soak | Soothe belly, calm cortisol, sleep deeply |
| **Night** | Foot or Bath Soak | Drain lymph, relax muscles, reset mood |

**Final Tip**

*Use a **glass or BPA-free bottle** for your infusions. Avoid* metal when using lemon or vinegar. Always sip slowly and stay mindful—this isn't a race, it's a ritual.

**Mason jars containing Cucumber mint (green tone), Berry lemon (pink/red), Turmeric tonic (golden hue), Salt soak jar with floral sprigs respectively.**

# Chapter 4

### The 21-Day Pink Salt Reset Plan

Most weight loss programs start with a diet.

This one starts with a **ritual**.

The *Pink Salt Reset* isn't just about dropping pounds, it's about realignment. Cellular hydration. Mineral restoration. Gut support. Hormone harmony. And yes, visible fat loss but without fighting your body.

This chapter gives you the entire 21-day roadmap—**step by step, week by week**—to transform how you feel, eat, and metabolize fat using one of nature's most underrated allies: **Himalayan pink salt**.

## What Is the Pink Salt Reset?

It's a simple 3-week routine that uses:

- Morning salt elixirs
- Infused detox waters throughout the day
- Nighttime tonics or soaks
- Optional light workouts
- A printable tracker for hydration, waist, mood, and energy

This plan gently supports:

- Weight loss
- Fat burning
- Digestive healing
- Hydration
- Stress reduction
- Hormonal rebalance

## Daily Core Routine (All 21 Days)

No matter which week you're in, these basics remain:

**Morning**

- **Drink your Pink Salt Elixir** (see Chapter 2)
- Wait 20–30 mins before food or coffee
- Gentle movement: stretching, walking, or journaling

**Midday**

- Sip **1–2 detox waters** infused with pink salt, berries, herbs, or citrus (see Chapter 3)
- Choose light, anti-inflammatory meals seasoned with pink salt
- Walk, stretch, or do yoga for 10–30 minutes

**Evening**

- **Golden Turmeric Tonic or Salt Sleep Water**
- Optional foot soak or bath with pink salt
- Reflect, breathe, and go screen-free 30 mins before bed

# What to Expect – A Gentle Journey

**Days 1–3**

- May experience mild headaches, tiredness, emotional waves
- Signs your body is recalibrating hydration, digestion, and mineral balance

**Days 4–7**

- Digestion improves, bloating decreases
- Energy stabilizes, cravings drop, sleep begins to deepen

**Week 2**

- Clearer skin, better mood, inches lost from belly
- Stronger metabolism and visible lightness in the face, gut, and waistline

**Week 3**

- Fat burning accelerates naturally
- You feel "tuned in"—clearer mind, deeper sleep, lighter body

Most people report less puffiness, weight loss, and renewed motivation

## Weekly Structure Overview

**Week 1: Cleanse & Hydrate**

**Theme:** Clear out stagnation, improve hydration, gently flush toxins

**Focus:**

- Morning salt elixir (¼ tsp pink salt + lemon)
- Cucumber Mint Flush in the afternoon
- Light meals: soups, broth, hydrating fruits, and leafy greens
- Avoid processed foods and refined sugar

**Goal:**

Reduce water retention, rehydrate cells, and reset digestion

**Optional Movement:**

10-minute stretch, light walk after lunch, gentle yoga

### Week 2: Detox & Activate

**Theme:** Activate metabolism, stabilize hormones, reduce inflammation

**Focus:**

- Add turmeric or ACV to morning or evening drink
- Midday berry lemon detox water
- Meals: protein-rich greens, light grains, pink salt roasted veggies
- Begin journaling energy, mood, cravings

**Goal:**

Turn on your body's natural fat-burning switches. Flatten

the belly.

**Optional Movement:**

Add 15–30 min brisk walks or home movement (low-impact HIIT, yoga)

**Week 3: Burn & Balance**

**Theme:** Maximize fat metabolism, support nervous system, create long-term balance

**Focus:**

- Double your water intake with infused salt waters
- Stick with golden turmeric tonic each evening
- Prioritize sleep, breathwork, and emotional regulation

**Goal:**

Deep cellular hydration, sustainable fat loss, nervous system calm

**Optional Movement:**

Add light strength work, dancing, or outdoor cardio (if energy allows)

## Daily Tracker Prompts (Included in Companion Printables)

Track the following each day to notice trends:

- Hydration (cups of infused water or elixir):
- Mood score (1–5):
- Sleep quality (hours + rating):
- Waistline (inches – once per week):
- Cravings (Low–Moderate–High):
- Energy levels (Morning / Afternoon / Evening):
- Notes or emotional shifts:

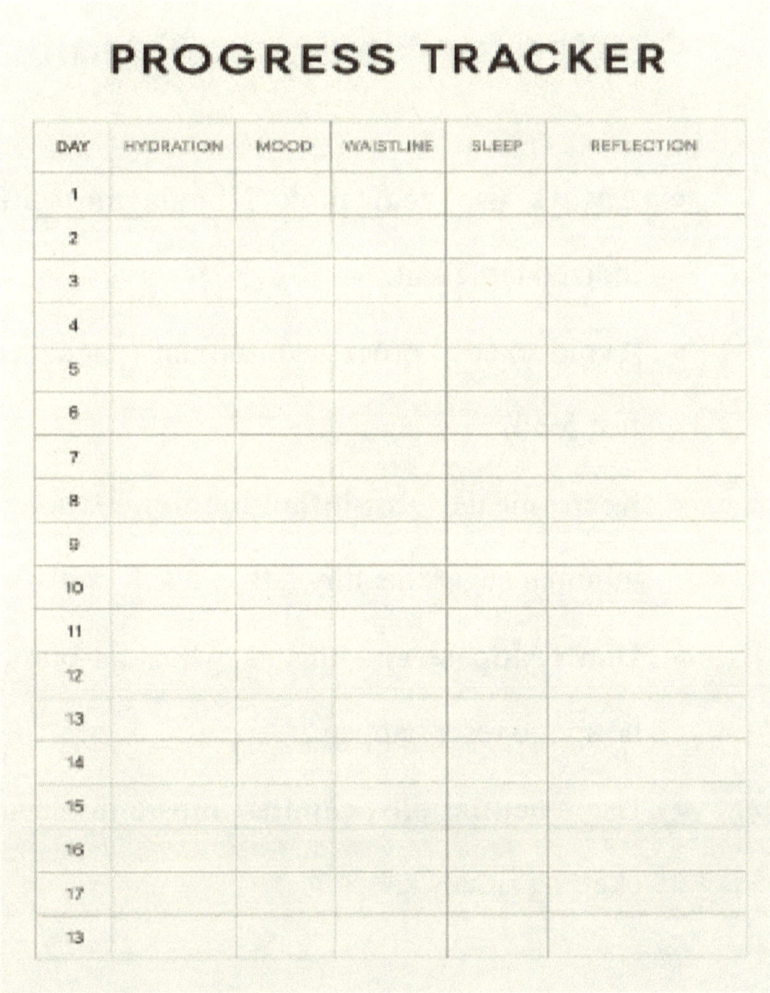

# PROGRESS TRACKER

| DAY | HYDRATION | MOOD | WAISTLINE | SLEEP | REFLECTION |
|---|---|---|---|---|---|
| 1 | | | | | |
| 2 | | | | | |
| 3 | | | | | |
| 4 | | | | | |
| 5 | | | | | |
| 6 | | | | | |
| 7 | | | | | |
| 8 | | | | | |
| 9 | | | | | |
| 10 | | | | | |
| 11 | | | | | |
| 12 | | | | | |
| 13 | | | | | |
| 14 | | | | | |
| 15 | | | | | |
| 16 | | | | | |
| 17 | | | | | |
| 13 | | | | | |

***A printable-style progress tracker graphic with rows for 21 days and columns for hydration, mood, waistline, sleep, energy, and reflection***

## Tips for Maximum Results

- Always use **real pink Himalayan** salt—never iodized table salt.
- Avoid excess processed sodium (packaged food, fast food).
- Keep meals **anti-inflammatory**: whole foods, minimal sugar, healthy fats.
- **Don't skip sleep**—this is when fat-burning and hormone reset happen.
- Use **essential oils, candles, music** to elevate your evening rituals.

## Real Talk: What If You Miss a Day?

You're human. Life happens.

If you miss a drink or indulge in something salty or processed, don't panic.

Just **resume your ritual the next day**. One moment doesn't undo the pattern. Healing is never linear.

**By Day 21, You May Notice:**

- 3–10 lbs lighter
- Decreased waist circumference
- Flatter belly
- Clearer skin
- Stronger sleep
- Fewer cravings
- Mental clarity
- Improved digestion
- More peace and energy

**Final Words Before the Reset Begins**

This is not a diet.

This is a *recommitment to yourself*.

With each glass, each breath, each moment of calm—you are signaling to your body:

*"I am safe now. You can let go."*

And in that letting go, fat is burned, inflammation fades, and your real vitality returns.

Let's begin.

# Chapter 5

**Daily and Weekly Meal Plans for Fat Loss with Pink Salt**

Let's get something straight: food is not your enemy.

But for far too long, wellness has been reduced to restriction—carb counting, macros, no-this, low-that. The result? Fatigue, cravings, rebound weight gain, and emotional burnout.

This chapter is your **escape from all that**.

Welcome to **salt-balanced nourishment**—simple meals and snacks that hydrate, energize, and reset your metabolism from the inside out. Every recipe here is packed with flavor, low on inflammation, and tuned to help you lose fat without feeling deprived.

# The Salt-Balanced Food Philosophy

The recipes and meal structure in this plan:

- Support digestion, metabolism, and blood sugar
- Hydrate the cells with trace minerals
- Reduce bloat, cravings, and emotional eating
- Encourage calm, focus, and fat burn through balanced electrolytes

You'll be eating **real food**: fresh produce, healthy fats, smart carbs, and natural proteins seasoned with just enough **pink salt** to nourish your adrenal glands and cellular hydration.

## Weekly Diet Structure

Each day in the 21-day plan includes:

**Morning Ritual Drink**

Start your day with your *Pink Salt Elixir*

(¼ tsp Himalayan salt + 8–12 oz warm water + lemon)

**Breakfast**

- Focus on smoothies, chia puddings, fruit bowls, or eggs—with a pinch of salt for adrenal balance

**Lunch**

- Think: balanced bowls, detox salads, roasted vegetables, lean protein, legumes—flavored with olive oil, herbs, and pink salt

**Dinner**

- Anti-inflammatory meals like grilled salmon, turmeric roasted sweet potatoes, sautéed greens, lentil soups, etc.

**Snacks**

Stay light: avocado slices with sea salt, salted nuts, herbal teas, dark chocolate with a pinch of salt, or a hydration fruit like watermelon with lime + pink salt

# Daily Sample Plan – Week 1: Beginner Focus

**Day 1**

**Morning Ritual:**

Pink salt + lemon elixir (warm water)

**Breakfast:**

Chia pudding made with almond milk, mixed berries, cinnamon, and a **pinch of pink salt**

**Lunch:**

Quinoa salad with chopped cucumber, fresh parsley, olive oil, lemon juice, and pink salt

**Dinner:**

Grilled salmon with sautéed spinach and turmeric-pink

salt roasted sweet potato cubes

**Snack:**

Cucumber slices with sea salt and fresh lime juice

**Day 2**

**Morning Detox Shot:**

Pink salt, apple cider vinegar, lemon juice, warm water

**Breakfast Smoothie:**

Spinach, frozen banana, flaxseed, vanilla protein, almond milk, pinch of pink salt

**Lunch:**

Chickpea and sweet potato curry (with turmeric, garlic, ginger, coconut milk, and pink salt) over brown rice

**Dinner:**

Zucchini noodles with tahini + pink salt dressing, sesame

seeds, and steamed broccoli

**Snack:**

Handful of pistachios or 2 squares of 85% dark chocolate sprinkled with sea salt

**Day 3**

**Morning Ritual:**

Pink salt + ginger + lemon water

**Breakfast:**

2 soft-boiled eggs with avocado slices and a dash of pink salt + turmeric tea

**Lunch:**

Lentil soup with cumin, garlic, carrots, and pink salt

**Dinner:**

Grilled tofu or chicken, kale sautéed in olive oil and salt, roasted carrots

**Snack:**

Watermelon with lime juice + pink salt (great post-workout)

**Day 4**

**Morning Elixir:**

Pink salt + lemon + cinnamon water

**Breakfast:**

Coconut yogurt parfait with fresh mango, chia seeds, and a sprinkle of pink salt

**Lunch:**

Baked falafel in lettuce wraps with tahini-pink salt drizzle

**Dinner:**

Baked cod with turmeric-spiced sweet potatoes and

asparagus

**Snack:**

Herbal tea + 1 tbsp almond butter with a pinch of pink salt

**Day 5**

**Morning Ritual:**

Pink salt + warm ginger water

**Breakfast:**

Overnight oats with oat milk, grated apple, cinnamon, pink salt, and walnuts

**Lunch:**

Cauliflower rice stir fry with pink salt, bell pepper, edamame, and coconut aminos

**Dinner:**

Ground turkey or veggie taco bowls with avocado,

shredded lettuce, salsa, and pink salt

**Snack:**

Orange slices with mint and a pink salt sprinkle

**Continue to Rotate for Days 6–21:**

Add seasonal swaps (butternut squash, berries, asparagus)

Adjust portion size based on energy needs

Keep salt moderate (not excessive)—let taste and mood guide you

## Tips for Food Success

- **Hydrate before eating:** 1 glass of water 15 mins before meals boosts digestion
- **Season with purpose:** Add salt *during* cooking not just at the table for even absorption
- **Stay light at night:** Focus on easy-to-digest dinners (soups, steamed veggies, broths)
- **Don't skip healthy fats:** Avocado, olive oil, tahini, and seeds help fuel hormones and satisfaction
- **Batch cook** on Sundays: Roast veggies, cook lentils, prep elixirs

## Optional Add-Ons for Advanced Days

- Add cayenne or ginger to your morning elixir

- Use pink salt in post-workout rehydration drinks
- Try intermittent "mini-fasts" between dinner and your next morning elixir (12–14 hours)

**Final Encouragement**

You are not dieting. You are **remineralizing**, rehydrating, and returning to a rhythm your body has long craved.

- As you follow this plan, notice:
- When your **cravings fade**
- When your **energy becomes steady**
- When your **clothes feel looser**
- When your **gut feels lighter**
- When your **face looks less inflamed**

These are not just signs of weight loss.

They are signs of **healing**.

# Chapter 6

**Pink Salt Recipes for Weight Loss and Gut Health**

Food can be a battleground or it can be your deepest medicine.

In this chapter, we return to the core of true nourishment: **healing warmth**, **replenishing minerals**, and **simple recipes** that soothe your gut, fire up your metabolism, and gently burn fat without stress, hunger, or sacrifice.

Using pink Himalayan salt as the foundation, the following recipes are designed to:

- Replenish **electrolytes**
- Soothe **inflammation**
- Support **gut lining repair**
- Calm the **nervous system**
- Stimulate **metabolism**

These recipes are perfect for in-between meals, post-workouts, cleansing days, or when you simply need comfort in a cup.

## Electrolyte Drinks & Salt "Mocktails"

Unlike sugary sports drinks or store-bought electrolyte powders, these drinks are **natural**, **clean**, and **functional**—perfect for restoring hydration, improving fat burning, and curbing cravings.

### Classic Mineral Hydration Elixir

**Ingredients:**

- 16 oz. filtered water (room temp or slightly warm)
- ¼ tsp pink Himalayan salt
- ½ lemon, juiced

- Optional: ½ tsp raw honey + 1 drop peppermint essential oil

**Instructions:**

- Stir salt into water until dissolved.
- Add lemon and other ingredients.
- Sip slowly throughout the morning.

**Citrus Salt "Mocktail"**

**Ingredients:**

- 12 oz sparkling water
- 1 tbsp fresh lime juice
- 1 tbsp fresh orange juice
- ⅛ tsp pink salt
- Mint leaves, crushed

**Instructions:**

- Mix all ingredients in a tall glass over ice.
- Stir and garnish with mint and a lime wedge.

**When to Use:**

Afternoon pick-me-up or pre-dinner appetizer to reduce cravings.

### Berry Electrolyte Sipper

**Ingredients:**

- 8–10 crushed raspberries or strawberries
- 10 oz coconut water
- ⅛ tsp pink salt
- Juice of ½ lemon

**Instructions:**

- Muddle berries in the bottom of a glass.
- Add coconut water, lemon, and salt.
- Stir and enjoy cold.

## Pink Salt Veggie Broths & Detox

# Soups

Perfect for gentle gut repair, hormone balancing, and bloat reduction.

### Alkaline Mineral Veggie Broth

**Ingredients:**

- 1 celery stalk
- 1 carrot
- 1 zucchini
- ¼ onion
- 1 clove garlic
- ¼ tsp turmeric
- ¼ tsp ginger
- ½ tsp pink salt
- 4–5 cups filtered water
- Handful of parsley

**Instructions:**

- Simmer all ingredients in water for 45–60 minutes.
- Strain and sip as a daily tonic.

**Use:**

Cleanse days, between meals, during illness or fatigue

**Pink Salt Detox Soup**

**Ingredients:**

- 1 tbsp olive oil
- 1 leek, chopped
- 1 cup chopped kale or spinach
- ½ cup broccoli
- 1 zucchini, diced
- 1 tsp pink salt
- Black pepper, to taste
- 4 cups water or veggie broth

**Instructions:**

- Sauté leek in olive oil.
- Add other ingredients and simmer for 20–25 minutes.
- Blend for a creamy texture or leave chunky.

## Bone Broths for Gut Lining Repair

Bone broths provide collagen, gelatin, and minerals that seal the gut lining, reduce inflammation, and support skin, joints, and hormone balance.

**Pink Salt Bone Broth for Gut & Fat Loss**

**Ingredients:**

- 2 lbs organic chicken bones or beef marrow bones
- 2 carrots, chopped
- 1 celery stalk
- 1 onion, halved
- 1 tbsp apple cider vinegar

- 1½ tsp pink salt
- Water to cover

**Instructions:**

- Place all ingredients in a large pot or slow cooker.
- Simmer on low for 8–24 hours.
- Strain and store in glass jars.

**To serve:**

Warm and sip with black pepper and a squeeze of lemon.

*Pink Salt Bone Broth for Gut & Fat Loss*

# Salted Herbal Teas for Metabolism & Mood

When pink salt is added to warm herbal teas, it **enhances absorption**, supports the nervous system, and improves metabolism especially when paired with adrenal or liver-supporting herbs.

**Ginger-Lemon Salted Tea**

**Ingredients:**

- 1 inch fresh ginger, sliced
- 2 cups water
- Juice of ½ lemon
- ⅛ tsp pink salt
- Optional: pinch of cayenne or turmeric

**Instructions:**

- Simmer ginger in water for 10 minutes.

- Strain, add lemon and salt.
- Sip warm in the morning or before meals.

**Lavender & Pink Salt Sleep Tonic**

**Ingredients:**

- 1 tsp dried lavender flowers
- 1 tsp chamomile
- 1½ cups hot water
- ⅛ tsp pink salt
- Optional: ½ tsp raw honey

**Instructions:**

- Steep herbs in hot water for 10 minutes.
- Strain and add pink salt.
- Drink 30–60 minutes before bed.

**Metabolism Green Tea with Pink Salt**

**Ingredients:**

- 1 green tea bag
- 1 cup hot water
- Juice of ¼ lemon
- ⅛ tsp pink salt

**Instructions:**

Steep green tea, then add salt and lemon.

Great in the morning or mid-afternoon to burn fat without caffeine crash.

**Final Guidance: Build Your Gut & Burn Plan**

**Use these recipes:**

- In between meals for digestive reset
- In place of caffeine or sugar cravings
- When bloated, anxious, or low-energy
- After workouts to restore minerals
- During illness or hormonal shifts

These drinks are gentle daily therapies that stack results

over time.

# Chapter 7

**Beauty & Body Rituals with Pink Salt**

Sometimes, weight isn't just physical. It's emotional. It's energetic. It's stuck in the skin, the lymph, the mind.

That's why true transformation must happen on both the inside and the outside.

Pink Himalayan salt—rich in minerals like magnesium, potassium, and calcium is not only a dietary ally, but also a powerful topical healer. When applied to the skin, soaked into the body, or massaged into targeted areas, pink salt helps **draw out toxins**, reduce **bloating and cellulite**, and restore your body's **natural glow**.

This chapter invites you into the spa of your own bathroom—no appointments, no products you can't pronounce. Just nature's purest salts, warm water, and a little time carved out just for you.

# Salt Baths for Lymphatic Drainage

A **lymphatic pink salt** bath is one of the fastest ways to reduce bloating, inflammation, and water weight. Your lymphatic system—your body's drainage and immune highway depends on **minerals + movement** to keep flowing.

When you soak in pink salt, it creates an **osmotic pull**: water leaves inflamed tissues and draws toxins out through the skin.

**Lymphatic Pink Salt Soak**

**Ingredients:**

- 1–2 cups pink Himalayan salt
- ½ cup baking soda
- 5 drops grapefruit essential oil (for cellulite + lymph)

- 3 drops eucalyptus or rosemary (for detox)
- Optional: dried rose petals or lavender buds

**Instructions:**

- Fill your bathtub with warm (not hot) water.
- Stir in all ingredients.
- Soak for 25–30 minutes in silence or calming music.

**Post-Bath Ritual:**

- Drink a glass of pink salt water or herbal tea.
- Dry brush skin before bed to continue drainage.

*A spa-inspired bath scene: A wooden spoon scooping pink salt into a white tub, rose petals floating, candlelight glowing nearby.*

## Salt Scrubs for Cellulite & Skin Glow

Pink salt makes an incredible **exfoliating scrub** that

removes dead skin cells, improves circulation, and helps **break up stagnant fat pockets** under the skin (cellulite). It also softens, brightens, and tones.

**Glow & Tone Pink Salt Scrub**

**Ingredients:**

- ½ cup pink salt (fine grain or crushed)
- ¼ cup coconut oil or olive oil
- 1 tbsp ground coffee (for extra cellulite action)
- 6 drops grapefruit or sweet orange essential oil

**Instructions:**

- Mix all ingredients in a small jar.
- Use in the shower on wet skin 2–3 times per week.
- Massage in circular motions, especially on thighs, arms, and belly.

**Pro Tip:**

*Scrub after workouts to increase blood flow and detox*

*effects.*

# Underarm Detox with Pink Salt Paste

Your underarms are one of the most toxin-heavy areas in the body where sweat, deodorant buildup, and lymph congestion gather.

This **salt paste detox** clears out odor-causing bacteria, **pulls toxins**, and helps reduce puffiness or tenderness in the armpits often caused by stagnant lymph.

**Pink Salt Detox Paste**

**Ingredients:**

- 2 tbsp pink salt (crushed or fine)
- 1 tbsp bentonite clay
- 1 tbsp apple cider vinegar

- 1 tbsp water or rosewater

**Instructions:**

- Mix to form a spreadable paste.
- Apply to clean underarms and let sit for 10–15 minutes.
- Rinse gently in the shower. Moisturize with coconut oil after.

**Use:**

2–3x per week, especially after workouts or sauna.

## Foot Soaks for Weight Loss, Hormone Balance & Stress

Your feet are rich with nerve endings, meridians, and detox pores. A pink salt foot soak can help reduce swelling, balance hormones, support adrenal recovery, and calm anxiety all of which affect **weight and fat storage**.

## Pink Salt Hormone-Balancing Foot Soak

**Ingredients:**

- ½ cup pink salt
- ¼ cup magnesium flakes (optional)
- 3 drops clary sage (hormone balance)
- 3 drops lavender (stress + sleep)
- Large basin of warm water

**Instructions:**

- Soak your feet for 15–30 minutes before bed.
- Breathe deeply, journal, or sip herbal tea while soaking.

**When to Use:**

- After emotionally draining days
- During PMS or hormonal fatigue
- Before bed for better sleep and recovery

# Optional Add-On: Salt-Infused Body Massage Oil

Mix pink salt (very fine) into a body oil like sesame or grapeseed for a **circulatory massage** that stimulates lymph, reduces soreness, and improves skin tone. Use upward strokes toward the heart.

## Summary Ritual Calendar

| Day | Morning | Midday | Evening |
|---|---|---|---|
| Monday | Dry brush | Body scrub | Pink Salt Bath |
| Tuesday | Stretch | Salt water flush | Foot Soak |
| Wednesday | Body oil | Salt elixir | Underarm |

|  | massage | | detox |
| --- | --- | --- | --- |
| Thursday | Glow scrub | Lymphatic walk | Salt soak |
| Friday | Dance/yoga | Hydration boost | Candlelit bath |
| Saturday | Massage oil | Detox tea | Salt + essential oil foot soak |
| Sunday | Rest | Gratitude journaling | Pink Salt Sleep Water |

**Final Reflection**

This is more than pampering.

These rituals remind your body that it's safe to release. To let go of inflammation. To stop holding water, toxins, and tension. To come back into balance.

When you treat your skin like it deserves to heal, your body responds with lightness, clarity, and glow from the inside out.

# Chapter 8

**The Science of Salt, Stress, and the Nervous System**

You don't just crave sugar because you're weak.

You don't store belly fat because you're lazy.

And your 3 p.m. crash isn't just about sleep or caffeine.

In truth, it often comes down to **mineral depletion**, **nervous system overload**, and **adrenal dysregulation** all of which are deeply tied to one misunderstood nutrient: **salt**.

In this chapter, you'll learn how pink salt especially in its unprocessed, mineral-rich form acts as a biological stabilizer, calming the chaos of modern stress, reducing emotional eating, and helping your body feel safe enough to let go of weight, inflammation, and stored tension.

# Cortisol, Adrenals & Salt

At the heart of stress lies a powerful hormone: cortisol.

Cortisol is your body's **fight-or-flight command** center. It raises blood sugar, increases fat storage (especially in the belly), and triggers cravings for high-calorie, salty, or sugary foods.

But here's the kicker: cortisol doesn't get activated just by fear. It gets triggered by:

- Skipping meals
- Poor sleep
- Chronic inflammation
- Overexercising
- Emotional tension
- **Electrolyte imbalance and dehydration**

Your **adrenal glands**, which produce cortisol and other vital hormones like aldosterone (regulates salt/water balance), are **mineral-hungry organs**. When you're under stress, they burn through sodium, magnesium, and potassium rapidly especially sodium.

When salt is low, your body reacts by:

- Elevating cortisol even more
- Holding onto fat for "safety"
- Triggering cravings for chips, fries, or snacks
- Causing fatigue, dizziness, irritability, and even insomnia

**Pink Salt to the Rescue:**

Pink Himalayan salt **replenishes adrenal minerals naturally**, helping your body feel safe, grounded, and nourished. It calms the fight-or-flight response, allowing your metabolism to shift from **storage** mode to **release**.

# Belly Fat & the Stress-Salt Cycle

Let's talk belly fat.

Fat around your midsection is biologically different than fat in other areas. It's rich in **cortisol receptors**, which means when your stress hormones rise, this is where your body stores fat first and releases it last.

The cycle looks like this:

1. Chronic stress → cortisol spikes
2. Cortisol → fat stored around belly + water retention
3. Fatigue/crashes → cravings for sugar/salt
4. Emotional eating → guilt → more cortisol
5. Repeat

It's not just emotional it's **biochemical**.

**Pink Salt's Role:**

- Restores **sodium/potassium** balance (vital for nerve and hormone signaling)

- Replaces the minerals lost during emotional or physical stress
- Signals safety to your body: "You are nourished. You can relax."
- Reduces need for artificial stimulants (caffeine, sugar, processed salt)

## Energy Crashes, Salt, and Blood Sugar Swings

Do you feel:

- Great in the morning but crash by 2–3 p.m.?
- Shaky or irritable between meals?
- Exhausted after workouts or long days?
- Like you "need something" but can't figure out what?

This isn't laziness. It's likely **adrenal stress + mineral**

**deficiency**.

Your nervous system and especially **your hypothalamic-pituitary-adrenal (HPA) axis** requires minerals like sodium, potassium, and magnesium to function smoothly.

When these are low:

- Blood sugar crashes faster
- Mood swings increase
- Brain fog intensifies
- Emotional eating patterns escalate

**Salt Hack for Energy Stability:**

A small pinch of pink salt in water **between meals or during energy dips** can stabilize blood pressure, curb cravings, and reboot your energy system **without caffeine or sugar**.

Even better? Combine it with lemon and a drop of peppermint or ginger essential oil for a full-body reset.

# Emotional Eating & Nervous System Dysregulation

Emotional eating isn't always about sadness.

It's often about **nervous system dysregulation** when your brain can't tell the difference between emotional threat and physical hunger.

The vagus nerve (which connects brain to gut) gets overwhelmed. Your body seeks fast fuel usually sugar, salt, or both.

But if you're **under-mineralized**, no amount of food will satisfy you.

**How Pink Salt Helps:**

- Satisfies hidden mineral cravings masked as hunger
- Sends safety signals via electrolyte correction
- Regulates dopamine (the brain's reward hormone)

- Prevents stress-induced binging by restoring calm

**Simple Emotional Eating Interrupt Tool:**

Before reaching for a snack when emotionally triggered, drink:

**"Nervous System Rescue" Salt Drink:**

- 8 oz warm water
- ¼ tsp pink salt
- ½ lemon
- 1 tsp raw honey
- 1 drop lavender essential oil (optional)

Sip it slowly. Breathe. Wait 10 minutes.

Notice how your craving softens.

## Nervous System Repair Rituals with

# Salt

Daily practices that pair well with pink salt for emotional and metabolic reset:

- **Morning salt-lemon elixir** while grounding barefoot outdoors
- **Midday pink salt mocktail** during a walk or journaling break
- **Nighttime golden turmeric tonic** with salt while reading or stretching
- **Salt baths or foot soaks** while listening to soothing music
- **Salt water affirmation ritual:**

As you sip, *say: "I am safe. I am supported. I am balanced."*

**Recap: Signs You May Be Mineral Depleted**

- ✓ Constant fatigue

- ✓ Sugar or salt cravings
- ✓ Headaches or brain fog
- ✓ Mood swings or irritability
- ✓ PMS or hormone crashes
- ✓ Belly fat or stubborn weight
- ✓ Emotional eating
- ✓ Sleep issues

If any of these feel familiar, pink salt may be your missing link.

Not a magic pill—just **missing information** your body's been waiting for.

**Final Words: From Fight-or-Flight to Flow**

Pink salt is not just food.

It's **feedback to your body**.

It tells your system, "You are nourished. You are safe."

And when your body finally hears that message, it stops

holding on—for dear life—to fat, fear, and fatigue.

You don't need more willpower.

You need more minerals.

More calm. More regulation.

More rituals that return you to **balance**.

# Chapter 9

## Troubleshooting & Adjustments

No journey especially one of healing is linear.

Even with the purest ritual, the cleanest food, and the most beautiful intentions, life can (and will) happen. You may travel, forget, bloat, or wonder if you're "doing it right." This chapter is here to answer those doubts.

Because pink salt is powerful but it's not one-size-fits-all.

Let's troubleshoot the most common questions and roadblocks, so you can keep going with ease, clarity, and grace.

## What If I Bloat?

Ironically, one of the most common early responses to the pink salt ritual is temporary bloating even though long-term, this practice helps reduce it dramatically.

**Why it Happens:**

- Your body is recalibrating its **fluid balance**
- Salt is pulling **water into your cells** (instead of leaving it trapped in tissues)
- You may be releasing stored toxins or trapped waste in the digestive tract
- Your **gut flora** is adjusting

**What to Do:**

- **Stay consistent for 3–5 days,** most bloating resolves naturally
- **Cut back salt slightly** (use 1/8 tsp instead of 1/4 tsp) and slowly increase over time
- Drink more **plain water** between salt drinks to flush lymph
- Add **lemon, ginger, cucumber, or mint** to infused water for support

- Try a **pink salt foot soak** or **dry brushing** to assist detox

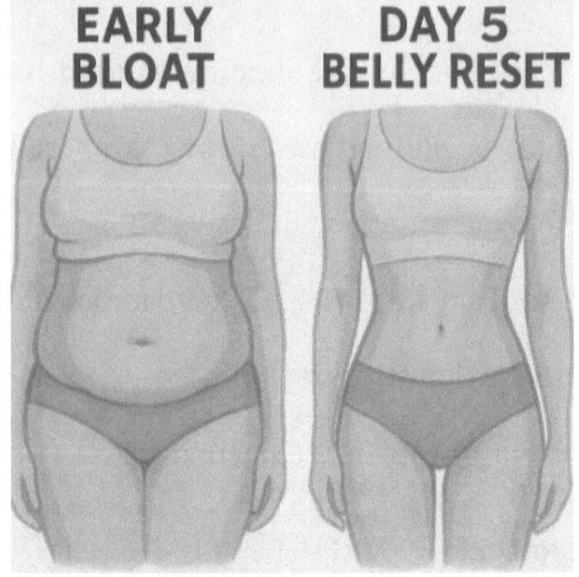

*"Early bloat" vs. "Day 5 belly reset" – showing initial puffiness and post-detox slim effect*

## How Do I Stay Consistent While Traveling or Busy?

Whether it's work, family life, or a trip, your rhythm might be interrupted. The key is not perfection it's **consistency without pressure**.

**On the Go Toolkit:**

- Pack a **small glass** jar with pink salt (pre-measured servings)
- Bring a **collapsible travel water bottle** for elixirs
- Use **fresh lemon packets** or travel-size ACV for your morning drink
- Download the **21-Day Tracker** to log meals and hydration
- If you skip a day: **resume the next day without guilt**

**Café/Restaurant Tips:**

- Order **warm lemon water** first thing in the morning
- Ask for **no added salt** in meals, then use your own pink salt
- Choose dishes with simple ingredients: steamed veggies, fish, rice, greens

*A travel kit small salt jar, lemon packet, foldable bottle, and tracker card*

## When Should I Increase or Reduce My Salt?

**Increase Salt If:**

- You're working out intensely (sweating a lot)
- You're transitioning off caffeine or sugar
- You feel dizzy or sluggish after meals

- You're fasting intermittently
- You're sweating in saunas or hot climates

**Reduce Salt If:**

- You feel bloated after multiple days
- You're getting headaches or dry mouth
- You eat a high-sodium packaged diet
- You have signs of **water retention** that don't resolve

**Customizing Your Ritual:**

- Start with **1/8 tsp daily** and increase to **1/4 tsp** based on response
- Use **half-strength drinks** in the evening or if sensitive
- Switch to **foot soaks** or **topical salt** scrubs on off days.

## Who Should Not Follow This Plan?

While pink salt is incredibly safe for most people, there are a few exceptions and it's important to respect them.

**Contraindications:**

- **People with kidney disease** (impaired sodium filtering)
- **Those with salt-sensitive hypertension** (consult your doctor first)
- **Individuals on sodium-restricted medications**
- **Pregnant women with preeclampsia** or water retention issues
- Anyone under 13 years old without medical supervision

**Modify With Guidance If:**

- You're pregnant or breastfeeding (use minimal salt, prioritize hydration)

- You're diabetic (pair salt drinks with protein or fiber to avoid spikes)
- You're post-surgical or on fluid restriction (consult your physician)

**When in Doubt:**

- Start with **external rituals** like foot soaks, body scrubs, or salt baths
- Consult a holistic nutritionist or physician familiar with electrolyte therapy

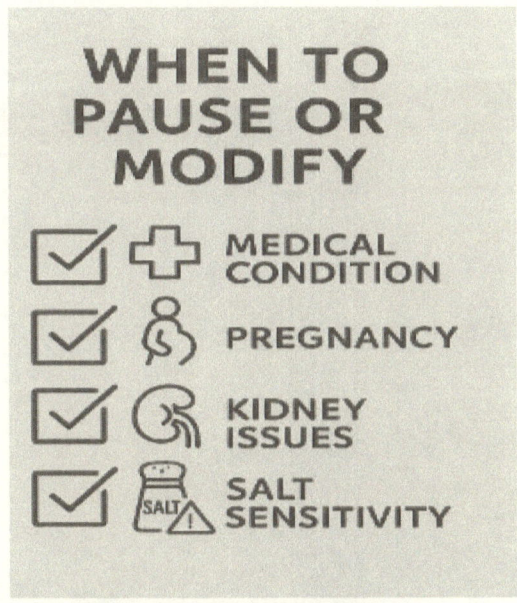

*Calm safety checklist*

**Closing Note: Trust Your Body's Voice**

This ritual is not about rules it's about **rhythm**.

And rhythm requires listening.

If you need less salt today, that's okay.

If your energy feels off, pause and check in.

If you're feeling vibrant, light, and focused—keep going.

Your body will speak.

Salt simply helps you hear it more clearly.

# Chapter 10

## Maintaining Results Long-Term

The 21-Day Reset was never the finish line. It was the foundation.

Now that your body is rehydrated, your cravings are calmer, your belly is lighter, and your energy feels stable—you might be asking:

**"What comes next?"**

The answer isn't more restriction. It's **rhythm**.

This chapter shows you how to stay aligned with the salt-balance principles you've learned without needing to "start over" or spiral back. Because once pink salt becomes part of your life, it anchors you whether you're thriving, traveling, healing, or simply maintaining.

# Using Pink Salt Post-Reset

Now that your system is recalibrated, your **salt needs may shift**.

You may not need the elixir daily, but strategic, weekly use will keep your:

- Digestion smooth
- Energy stable
- Skin glowing
- Hormones regulated
- Adrenals supported

## How to Maintain Momentum (Sample Weekly Plan)

| Day | Morning Ritual | Hydration Support | Night Ritual |
|---|---|---|---|

| Day | | | |
|---|---|---|---|
| Monday | Salt + Lemon Elixir | Cucumber Mint Water | Foot Soak |
| Wednesday | Salt + ACV Water | Ginger + Citrus Mocktail | Lavender Tea + Salt |
| Friday | Detox Tonic | Anti-Bloat Berry Water | Salt Bath |
| Sunday | Rest Day | Coconut Salt Sipper | Golden Milk + Pink Salt |

**Pro Tip:**

*Let your body guide your dosage. Some weeks you may crave more; other weeks, less. That's balance.*

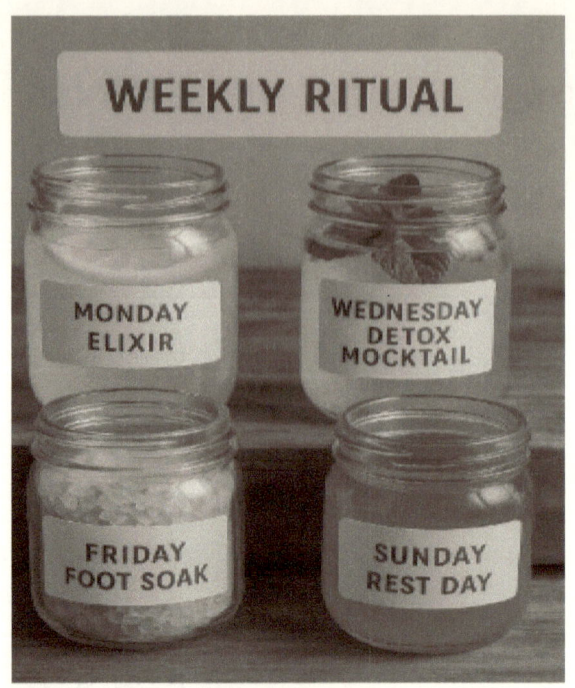

*Weekly ritual grid layout with labeled jars*

## Build Your Own Rituals

The best ritual isn't the perfect one. It's **the one that meets you where you are**.

Here's how to create sustainable pink salt habits that work for your lifestyle.

### Morning Grounding Ritual

- **When to use:** Low mood, sluggish mornings, hormonal imbalance
- **Ingredients:** 8 oz warm water, ¼ tsp pink salt, juice of ½ lemon, ginger or ACV
- **Add-ons:** Breathe for 3 minutes, journal one line, stretch arms overhead
- **Purpose:** Hydrate + awaken digestion

### Mindful Eating Ritual

- **When to use:** Before meals to curb overeating
- **Steps:**
  1. Sip 5 oz pink salt water 10 mins before eating
  2. Lightly season your meal with pink salt while thinking: "This food is healing me."
  3. Eat slowly. Notice texture, flavor, gratitude.

## Night Recovery Ritual

- **When to use:** After long days, workouts, arguments, tech overload
- **Options:**
  - Warm salt bath with lavender
  - Salt tea + peppermint oil on temples
  - Foot soak + journaling

*"Morning Salt Ritual," "Meal Salt Ritual," "Evening Reset*

# Salt-Balance Eating Principles

You don't need to "stay on a diet." You just need to eat in **alignment with your body's mineral rhythm**.

**Core Guidelines for Long-Term Salt-Balance Nutrition:**

**Prioritize:**

- Real whole foods: fruits, leafy greens, quality fats
- Naturally salty foods: seaweed, celery, miso, olives
- Mineral-rich hydration: lemon water, herbal tea with pink salt
- Salt your meals mindfully (during cooking > after)
- Add potassium-rich foods to balance: banana, sweet potato, lentils

**Limit:**

- Refined table salt (sodium chloride with no trace minerals)

- Processed foods with hidden salt + sugar + MSG
- Salty carb-sugar combos (chips, fries, fast food)
- Skipping meals—leads to cortisol + salt depletion
- Over-restrictive "clean" eating that creates mineral imbalances

## Pink Salt + Potassium Balance = Metabolic Magic

Your cells crave **sodium-potassium balance**. Pink salt gives you natural sodium. Foods like avocado, greens, and bananas provide potassium.

**Together, they**:

- Lower inflammation
- Help cells absorb nutrients
- Regulate fluid balance
- Maintain a steady mood and energy curve

- Trigger fat burning without stress

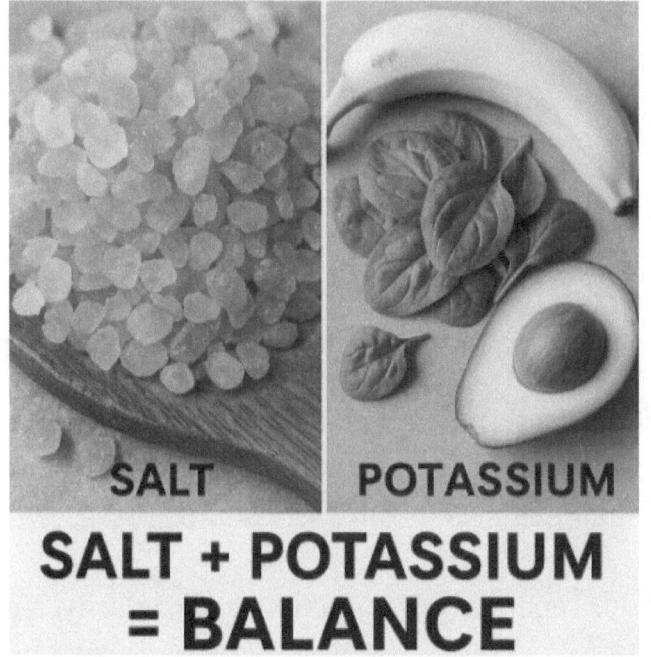

*Left – pink salt, Right – banana, spinach, avocado*

**Final Reflection: The Ritual Is Now Inside You**

You've made it through the reset. You've done more than "burn fat"—you've burned **old patterns**.

You now understand:

- Why you craved what you did

- Why you held weight you didn't want
- Why hydration was missing from healing
- Why **salt** was never the enemy—just the missing key

Keep this book nearby. Revisit the recipes. Keep jars of salt and lemon within reach. But most importantly—**keep choosing rituals over rules.**

Ritual heals what rules never can.

Your energy. Your belly. Your clarity. Your nervous system.

It's all responding to your care.

You don't have to start over.

You just have to keep showing up—one glass at a time.

# Glossary of Key Terms

A beginner-friendly guide to commonly used words in this book so readers feel confident and empowered, not overwhelmed.

**Electrolyte Balance**

The ideal ratio of minerals like sodium, potassium, magnesium, and calcium that keeps your cells hydrated, muscles functioning, and energy stable.

**Osmosis**

The movement of water from areas of low concentration to high mineral concentration. In the body, this explains how pink salt draws water into your cells for optimal hydration.

**Solé Water**

A saturated pink salt solution (typically 1 tsp of salt dissolved in 1 cup of water, diluted before use). Used for deep mineral replenishment and adrenal support.

**Adrenal Fatigue**

A controversial but widely recognized term describing low energy, cravings, and hormonal imbalance caused by prolonged stress and depleted cortisol regulation.

**Cellular Hydration**

Not just drinking water, but getting it into the cells—requires salt (sodium) and potassium to cross cell membranes and hold moisture where it's needed.

**Gut-Brain Axis**

The communication system between your gut and nervous system. Emotional eating, bloating, and mood shifts are all regulated through this connection.

**Thermogenesis**

The process of heat production in the body that can help boost metabolism. Spices like cayenne or pink salt paired with warm elixirs may encourage gentle fat burning.

**Mineral Burnout**

A state of low energy, cravings, and fatigue caused by long-term depletion of essential trace minerals—often corrected by consistent pink salt intake.

# Acknowledgments

To the quiet mornings and the healing rituals that whispered, "*Start here.*"

To every woman who ever felt bloated, tired, confused, or defeated by her own body—I wrote this for you.

Thank you to my readers, friends, and early testers who believed in the power of pink salt before the world caught on. Your stories, feedback, and transformations gave this book its heartbeat.

www.ingramcontent.com/pod-product-compliance
Lightning Source LLC
Chambersburg PA
CBHW030555080526
44585CB00012B/380